GW01374863

Need a new notebook? Visit smartbookx.com

23056522R00054

Printed in Great Britain
by Amazon